PORTALS

Poems
by Charles Wm. Preble

CUP AND SPIRAL BOOKS
MINNEAPOLIS MINNESOTA

For Jana

Forever and forever

CONTENTS

Awakening	2
After August	3
He Loved His Church	4
Alone in the Alone	6
Annunciation	8
Thusness	9
On Self-Importance	10
Azure	11
The Balvenie	12
The Blessing	14
Cardinal	15
The Charcoal Drawing of a Cat's Head My Mother Drew	16
Do Not Hasten the Day	17
Venus	18
Family Homes	19
Black and White Photograph, 1934	20
He Ate and Drank the Precious Words	21
Henslow's Sparrow	22
Mountain Moments	25
Hidden Pond	26
Homer	28

Jana, Love	31
The Last Craft	32
Mi Pueblo	34
Moonrise, Hernandez, New Mexico, 1941	36
Night Voices	38
1942: What I Knew	40
November Tenth	42
Patient and Hidden	43
Perfect Attendance	44
Persona and Person	46
The Prairie Hawk	47
The Reunion	48
Seamus Heaney	51
Singular	52
Song of Longing	55
Five Sea Interludes	56
Goshawk	60
A Thing with Feathers	62
Still, as a Child	63
The Vanishing Art of Feather Reading	64
Paradise	65
Vissi d'arte, Vissi d'amore	66

I Will Leave It Free And Open And Unnamed	67
Wayfarer	68
Sisyphus	69
Mercy	70
What Do You Bear?	73
What Is Poetry, and Where Do I Fit In?	74
Why We're Here	77
The Wind in the Night	78
To Wonder	80
Like a Bell	82
Itasca	84
While I Have Time	85
Mortal,	87
Portal	88
This Day	90
Acknowledgments	93

Thy life's a miracle. Speak yet again.

King Lear, IV.vi.55

Awakening

There is only
this day.

This day
carries no record
of my neglect
nor any request
for my regrets

This winter,
so long,
so deep,
shall not last.

Nineteen below,
this morning,
the sky
blinding—
a simple summons.

After August

It is the last of summer's
haze, as the earth's head turns,
and the autumn equinox nears

The leaves on this white ash
are now pale, having lost their viridescence,
left with only a hint of future gold.
A reluctant few relinquish their hold
and fall as the slant sun catches them.
The light plays like a remembrance,
and the day now seems as light
as an old memory.

This day does not require, insist
or demand. Yet, let this remaining light
be. Let it be. My reverie is of no other
world, nor of an other time, but of this precious
here, as passing as it is, as real as it is,
as lasting as it is. *Here.* Let it be.

He Loved His Church

He loved his church
from the first time he entered
at the age of ten at ten
in the morning. The sun-full
east window with its luminous
reds and blues was the only light
in the church.

It was open at all hours, and when
he was alone, and most especially
when he was lonely, he would come in
to be held in its light, its color,
and even in its dark tallowy scent.
He was in an-other place called *holy*.
Bewildered, he had found his sanctuary,

this place of silence.
His favorite time was the space before the service
began. Then slowly, in a low polyphony,
the organist played a prelude, maybe
Duruflé. He was embraced in the music just
as he always was by the soulful women's
chorus, in Debussy's *Nocturnes*.

Even the liturgy invited him
into a world of beauty in the language
of Herbert and Donne, and hymns
and chants ancient, medieval,
and modern. Here he found
the beauty of holiness, and
the holiness of beauty.

The priest spoke
without sanctimony or rant.
Never a word that you were
a bad person who must be saved.
What he did hear was that
God was love, and love
was all he ever needed to know.

Alone in the Alone

Dark and light clouds
brush the cerulean sky.

Shadows graze
the terra cotta sand.

The sagebrush roots
plumb their dry space.

The dark-brown mesa
rises in the east.

The horizon deludes
the mind's clear eye.

The abandoned adobe
remains, plaster crumbled,

windows open, broken,
door long removed,

waiting, waiting, waiting
for the unknown guest.

Empty stillness in this
desert place, where

loneliness is welcomed
and solitude is the reward.

The clouds wander on.
They leave no rain.

Annunciation

        Sun filled fall day.
   Be still. Still as the starling
       in this poplar. Still
    is the way here. Still sees
    without belief. The leaves
    glisten, listen to the eyes.
        You are free,
 says the voice, which is mine.
     The words are not mine.
I cannot speak. Silence is still
  in the whisper of the leaves.

Thusness

Of course you cannot see
from here to there,
even on a clear day.
Tomorrow lies hidden,
is, at best, unclear.

Time was when you never
worried about it. Time was
too important to waste, best
hurry along. Too long
it has taken to be enfolded
in the eternity of this moment.

                See

this pink-breasted chickadee.
She feeds at your window.

On Self-Importance

I walk in the early evening light,
down the gravel drive. I stop
to wait for the moon, soon to rise.

The drive lies beside a wilderness;
refuge for families of deer,
grouse, pheasant, and wild turkey.

Then I see, thirty feet away, a fawn,
maybe a week or two old, caught
in the grip of the barbed wire fence.

The more it struggles, the more the spikes
dig in with their crucifying hold.
The more it strives, the more frantic

it becomes. Paralyzed,
I wait. But then I witness
a wonder: the fawn breaks free,

shakes itself as if it's only grazed —
in a quick moment, looks at me —
then is off into its underbrush home.

Beyond the fence, out in the cornfield
come the raucous songs of coyotes.
The moon begins its rise.

Azure

All is suspended
as Venus appears
where tomorrow she will be joined
by the thinnest crescent moon.

It is the part of the day my father
seemed to live the whole day for.
Each time was a first time —
those moments after he stopped
working, sweating, and swearing.

Slowly on the russet wall
the shadows rise as the sky
turns toward gentleness, is
more blue than at any other time
of the day — the purest azure.

If I come close to missing him
it is now, at this quiet time of day,
when words between us
were benign or nonexistent,
and we knew each other
as father and son.

The Balvenie

— For Wes

Late July, in the afternoon, we sit
in the shade sipping *The Balvenie*,
enjoying the aroma of hollyhocks
in bloom, and the thrum of bees,
a bit tipsy with nectar. We reminisce
about backpacking south of Ajo
in the Sonoran desert, with our
single malt whiskey from Spey,
and the deepest star-full night
when the scorpion got loose
in your jeans.

Today we don't give a damn
that rattlesnakes can see
with their eyes closed. We're
watching a *mantis religiosa*
poised on the red sugar
feeder, waiting for his prey
before he loses his head
to his true love.

Here the blue and lavender
hummingbirds hover
and dart with such ease.

Maybe they still remember
their five-hundred-mile flight
over the Gulf of Mexico.

Why would they ever
want to stop.

The Blessing

In the darkest quiet of night,
hiding the light of moon and star,
it came, choosing its own hour,

as we lay in our other world;
then, at the break of day,
a fresh loft of snow picks up

the sun's slant light,
and on our doorstep
lay a spray of scarlet, held

its chilling-white embrace,
as large as a human
heart, no sign

of feather or fight, no
mark of fur or struggle; solely
this blood blessing.

Cardinal

Each day I fill the feeders,
and the bluejays and starlings,
the nuthatches and chickadees
all come.

I would feed them all,
each one, every day,
always, hoping
that you, too, might be fed.

The Charcoal Drawing of a Cat's Head My Mother Drew

The rendering is held
mid-paper with all its
cat-ness contained
in the head alone. Whiskers

and ears alert, its eyes
pierce mine, hold me
in its gaze and I get
a glimmer that it can see

my mother's eyes
as she held me
on my first day, and beheld
me in unspoken wonder.

Do Not Hasten the Day

How shall I appear on that
last day. Shall I be in a gown
glowing white. I hope not,
for I have another thought

of what glory is about:
I no longer lust for a body
taut, sinewy, and strong,
nor would I hide these

bulges and sags that come
with gravity and age, nor
would the finest merino robe
seem seemly to hide life's

shame or pain. Yes, I would
my sins be shriven. But if I
be riven and examined
to the last atom, like Adam

I must give thanks for what
I have been given. Nothing
would fit me better than
to be found as a ludic child,

if wizened and gray, naked
at play, giving joy to the one
who made me exactly this way.

Venus

At dusk, as I walk the homeward path,
the gravel grates beneath my feet,
and my head is weary of wasp-like
quibbles; as each seeks a rest
that does not exist and festers
in others with an endless whine.
God, help me.

At once she appears, hair dark
and full, robed in twilight pinks
and blues, with eyes afire, she draws
my grumblings into a ledger,
then tears the book in half and half
again, and throws them to the wind,
These, she says, *are nothing*!

She leaves in the fullness of silence;
and in that wholeness, a new moon rises.

Family Homes

> — *after Adam Zagajewski*

The grand Victorian mansion
with its high balcony and tall columns,
where there was no room you would call
your own, and where behind it a giant

green pepper tree grew; and much farther back,
beyond the coach house and servants' quarters,
was the derelict garden with an apricot tree
wanting to bloom and the shiplapped toolshed
you swept out and made your own — all torn down
now, all now macadamed, smothered earth.

Then to the high desert into the adobe
ranch house, lost alone on a hill, afloat in miles
and miles of sagebrush where coyotes yipped,
and rattlesnakes hid, where you would walk
and walk amid the scent of sage and the desert rose,
now all lost in a thicket of look-alike homes.

Back then, to escape the desert heat,
you would drive to the ocean cove with friends,
listening to Debussy and Ravel in the dark,
talking until two or three a.m.; driving back
far too late, your folks worried sick.
Up before dawn and out all day for the hunt.
Not coming back until dusk. With each of them
you were so thick. And you left them
without a thought, lived as a stranger.
But these were your family homes.

Black and White Photograph, 1934

The man behind the counter is my father,
age thirty-five. Hair slicked down
like Rudolf Valentino, sure was
the ladies' man. Behind him are oil paintings,
water colors, and nineteenth-century
tintypes. Inside the counter is old gold
jewelry, antique sterling flatware, crystal
and cut glass stemware. He started buying
and selling antiques during the Depression
going door to door after the real estate
business bottomed out. No handouts
or WPA for him. He was his own man,
thank you. Left school and home
in the eighth grade and set out on his own.
Roustabout, acrobat. Did handstands
on the wings of biplanes for the crowds
at county fairs. Didn't believe in
the preachers' God, although his vocabulary
expressed a cursing knowledge of theology.
After two wives, he dated my grandmother,
until he met her teenage daughter. Two
years later, I was born, his only son. I grew up
to be a priest.
      Oh, father.

He Ate and Drank the Precious Words
— from Emily Dickinson, #1593

Awake at two,
the light drifts down the narrow hall
leading him to the sun room,
full of the moon, the moon that shall
never wax or wane, the moon
transfiguring field and sky,
lighting volumes of verse
lining the east wall.

    The moon glows
    through the tall window in the high
    ceilinged bedroom where she sits
    dressed in a white night gown
    and blue mantle, her dark red hair
    unbound.

    And as he stands, still as a book
    on a shelf, she returns
    to the paper on her small table
    and writes — her words as fierce
    as her eyes:
        And this Bequest of Wings
        Was but a Book — What Liberty
        A loosened Spirit brings —

He sits, her book
open on his knees, —
its pages wings.

Henslow's Sparrow

Just south of the gravel drive
where the grass grows guarded
by the barbed wire fence I am
an intruder on bent knee,
weeding a derelict flower bed,

avoiding the lilies, gladiolas,
and tulips, long since stopped
blooming. I pull up dandelions,
thick grass, and thistles
each clinging to the rock-hard clay

reluctant to relinquish its hold.
Then, before me, in the smallest
woven-grass nest on the ground
appear, begging, four beaks. And
I have nothing to give them.

And I have ruined their refuge.
And the next day, when I return
a small, brown blur scuttles
away from the nest, straight
into the thick grass, hidden

under the fence. I can't tell
if it is a parent or a rodent;
But, the following day
the chicks sleep unharmed. Later,
that day, their nest is bare.

Days later, just beyond the nest,
on the barbed wire fence,
the smallest brown sparrow, with its
defiant cricket-like whistle,
raises its beak to the sky.

Mountain Moments

I can't go back to that Easter
before the war began,
when we three sat on the ground
in the dappled light
under big-cone spruce
in the mountains
east of Santa Ana.
The sky was clear,
the sun warm,
the breeze gentle
with the scent of spruce
and fried chicken.
My grandmother,
her wild red hair,
my young mother,
and I were there.
We were all giddy,
which is an odd word,
'possessed by a god.'
We were beguiled by beauty,
by being together,
by one another,
by not knowing any better.

Hidden Pond

Eager to find a place
away, alone, I take
the well mown walk

behind the row of cabins
to an almost hidden trail,
veiled in green light;

a path made soft
by the russet needles of pine
and marked by gnarled roots

winding through the earth,
and, on either side,
a dense underbrush

that causes me
to walk as if in
a cloistered space;

and I know that I enter
a portal to another realm —
glacier carved, spring fed —

where gray wolf and deer
slake their thirst;
a quiet, sunlit pond,

where a beaver swims
slow circles, and, with a flip
of his tail and a splash, dives

only to rise again
and sees where I stand.
Another flip, another splash,

a longer look, and then
continues his swim,
as I lie down on the bank

and watch the tall pines
swaying in the gentle wind
and listen to their fluent

whisper-song bidding me
to rest my back, content
with what I know of heaven.

Homer

When the hot winds howled down the canyons,
you came, a pack slung over your shoulder,
which held a notebook, bedroll, socks, and underwear,
and probably a split of Jim Beam.

My father told me your name was Homer; that
you were a drifter; that he'd given you work
to do, paid you cash. No telling, my father said,
when you'd hit the road again.

That night you stayed in the old shiplapped
garden shed; swept it out and laid down
your bedroll. You were there when I came home
from school; you'd just finished for the day,

had rolled a Bull Durham and sat outside the shed,
with time to talk. Like you had all the time
in the world. You asked about school, and I said
I hated it. Didn't care much for it myself, you said.

I wanted to know about the places
you'd been and which you liked the best.
Everywhere, you grinned, then you told me
anywhere in the West, and on you went

with stories of old Santa Fe, El Paso,
Monterey, of fishing for trout
in the high Sierras. You wanted your feet
to carry you wherever you would go.

I would hurry home each day to talk with you,
and you had time to listen, and always a story.
I would stay with you until Mother called me
in for supper, almost always without Father.

There was a day when I came home; a day
when school had not been so bad, and
you were gone — left that morning
without a whisper— never saw you again.

Father and I would never learn to speak together
of what mattered most. Except, near the end
as I was departing, I reached out to him
and he returned the hug,

Our eyes very moist,
but not another word.

Jana, Love

The lung cancer metastasized
into her bones, and at the age of sixty-four,
my mother, given months to live,

was moved into long term care
where her roommate screamed
all day and all night. You were

the one who answered the question
we did not know how to ask:
*Mamacita will come to live
and die with us.* She agreed
and an air ambulance carried
my mother from Phoenix

to Reno. All her life she feared
flying, but this, she said, was bliss.
Over the months every hope

of a cure was dashed,
and it was you who became the daughter
she always wanted; it was you

who helped me with her at night;
it was you who showed
our young daughters

that dying is part of living
and it was love
that did the heavy lifting.

The Last Craft

With all of the intricacy of
a goldfinch nest but without
the finch's finesse, I attend
to the final craft. I sort
through memory's dissimilar
threads and yarns, and find
some that fit together as if
by divine fiat. Others, of course
were pure gossamer,
blown away by any zephyr.
Then there are the other parts;
old buttons and badges, ribbons
and medals, and parchments,
which used to mean so much,
but, as I sift through them,
I wonder what was I thinking.
Even so, I keep them.

I continue
to weave without the need
for warp and woof,
a kind of collage. As some old folks
will do, I save bits and pieces that I
store here and there with no apparent
sequence or direction even though some
order now would save me
from puzzled choices later on.

Yet I attend the final craft,
sure that I'll remember
how each part fits together.

I am touched by my sureness.
In my older years, I'm impressed
by my belief that the pattern
will be found.

Mi Pueblo

— For J

I will take you there, where the *piñon*
burns at night, where you shall taste its sweet
smell; where the aspen turns golden,
and where the clear sky of autumn speaks
the only truth.

North of the plaza, on *El Camino del Rio*,
we will walk along the adobe wall
to where it is broken by a turquoise
wooden door, lift the wrought iron latch,
and enter the flagstone courtyard, breathing in
the aroma of Anaheim peppers roasting.
Under the *ramada* the table is made
ready for us: *Chiles rellenos con queso*, green fire,
hot *sopapillas* with bees' milk to quench
the flame. Afterward we will walk in the shade
of giant cottonwood trees to the *Rio Chama*,
to lie down on its bank, joined, to learn the songs
of wind and water.

When the sun sets our faces ablaze,
we turn to the east
to watch the mountaintops change
into *el Sangre de Christo* and we will stroll
to Estrelita's bookstore, where her *kiva* glows
welcome to guests. Estrelita, ever present

angel of the printed world, offers books for the soul's
healing. Wisdom's smile greets every quest,
and if we don't know our want, we have only to ask,
for Estrelita knows our deeper wish.

When the evening bells have rung
we will enter *la Iglesia de San Pasqual.*
Pasqual, the patron of the kitchen, always
there to feed the soul; he knows God speaks
most clearly in the voice of silence.
The *santos* greet us, carvings of love,
each with its own *niche* in the walls,
their words need no translators. Votives
with soft tongues of fire whisper of pleas left,
and desires left to hope's surprises.

And we shall stand
under the clarity of the stars, our mothers
and our fathers, and watch the moon rise
over *mi pueblo,* and hold each other,
then lead each other as we disappear
into that clear night, our spirits filled
with what we have been given.

Moonrise, Hernandez, New Mexico, 1941

— *Ansel Adams*

Tomorrow night our loved ones will sing and dance
the songs on accordion and violin; the songs
we taught them. Their heels will scuff and drum
the earthen floor. Their sweaty faces will gleam
in light from candle and kerosene lamp.

> *Crosses and headstones glow in the sun's*
> *late descent. Pink pastels cover our snow*
> *peaked mountains and the clouds beyond.*
> *The cottonwoods, their gold now shed,*
> *stand, stark harbingers. Belted kingfishers*
> *fly low and fast over the Chama river;*
> *their rapid rattles announce the feast.*

We live within our loved ones: they breathe
us in the air, they work the dirt where they buried
us. They hear us in the wind, smell us
in the scent of piñon fire. We visit them
in dream and reverie. In them we laugh and rage.
When they grieve, our tears fall. When they wake,
and when they sleep, our warm blood flows in them.
These nights and days are made for them.

> *Tomorrow in the church of San Jose,*
> *Mass will be said, songs of our dear*
> *ones will be sung, votives lit, and*
> *incense shall rise, lifting our hearts.*

We are ready for the triduum: Dias
de los Muertos. *Their favorite foods
have been prepared: tamales, mole,
and pan de muerto. These nights and days
are made for them. What they cannot
eat we shall consume.*

Night Voices

Your soul is nested
   in dark light,

its being, its own wonder,
   reflected in this stark night.

The winds each write
   their verses in flight.

Close by the owl softly moans,
   its wings alive to the beat,

the knocking screen door,
   with raw fiddle whine, keeps time.

Then a stillness
   as if a deep breath is taken

before the final line is read. All the while
   you listen, as yet an other

night voice shifts its throat
   to tell its own reverie.

Their voices lift like birds
   in starlit migration.

O seductive night voices:
    O enfolded souls:

each seeks its home
    where none has ever been.

1942: What I Knew

I watched the Japanese planes bomb Chinese cities,
and refugees flee on foot away from their homes,
the German army invade Paris with tanks
and goose-stepping troops on the newsreels.
Each night we gathered around the radio
and listened to the news.
I knew war.

Pearl Harbor was struck. There was talk
they might attack Long Beach, only fifteen
minutes from our home. Reports of submarines
sighted just off our coast. At night
I heard the booms of naval bombardment. We had
air raid drills in school, and blackouts at night.
I knew fear.

Early that March morning while it was still dark,
we loaded up our 1940 black DeSoto sedan. As Father
drove us through the mountains into the desert,
I slept on the back seat. He parked the car on an old
dirt road and awakened me. I saw pastel blues,
turn into rich hues of azure. Then a dazzling prism
of yellows and reds, and the glimpse of an eye of fire.
As the desert awakened
I knew beauty.

In this beauty, far from war, Father and I
collected pieces of dried sagebrush
and mesquite. Father fixed a small fire.
Then, on a cast iron griddle, Mother prepared
a breakfast of eggs, bacon and hash browns
with scallions. My favorites.
I knew love.

November Tenth

Around three a.m. it came
out of the southwest, took aim,
and we got the best—ten inches
by ten; by afternoon, seventeen.
The wind swung its way in
and twirled white drifts, and left us
alone in another world.

Feverishly, even joyously,
the juncos and nuthatches
feed. Three cardinals return, as if
they need this day, this snow,
this island home.

Our have-tos and to-dos are scrapped.
The scent of pinto beans and smoked
ham hocks simmering fills the air,
and the fire in the Jøtul keeps us inside.

Our friends—Jane, Emily, Seamus,
and Robert—wait
on the shelves, say *Come, sit down.*
This day, this world, is meant for you.

We two savor our Earl Grey
and our thoughts slow down in this dream
of silence and simplicity. Even though
we know that this, also, shall
pass, we smile at each other
as the world beyond us hurries in its whirl.

Patient and Hidden

At the end of the township
road you might find us, but
each year the entrance
becomes more obscure,
as the trees grow more dense,
like an uncharted somewhere
on the edge, as a river runs
between wildness and field,
between field and wood.

The world moves on in its
harried way beyond us,
as if we are part of a sphere
that has long passed away.

Guests immediately sense
this is a different world:
How did you find this spot?
when it seems to us as if
it was always waiting for us.

As the decades appear
and vanish, we are given
a sense of being outside time,
out of step, in an epoch
of our own
other world,
patient and hidden

Perfect Attendance

If the day had not been
startlingly clear,
you would not
have taken
the path,
or followed
the course
of the wash
deepening
into the arroyo.

If the day had been warmer
you would not have sat
on the stone,
felt the warmth
of the winter sun
on your back,
or smelled
the freshness
of the desert
morning.

If you had not looked up
at the coral limestone ledge,
perhaps two arm-lengths
from your head,
you would not
have seen
the one nested
in its reticence,
perfectly coiled.

Persona and Person

He put on the dark grey worsted suit.
He loved its honest texture, and the pure
black shirt, with its wide white collar.
It all fit so well. It was so sacerdotal.
Trying it on was one thing,
being seen in it another.

The deference he received never fit him
very well. When he wanted most to show
he really cared, he heard: *Father,
you wouldn't understand. You're
a priest.* It was a curse. Really.

As time went on he would let it slip:
the thing, the very thing one
would not expect a priest to say,
and utter it with such insouciance,
that notice was immediate.
And then he heard:

You're not like all the rest.
And that was all
he ever wanted to be.

The Prairie Hawk

Last night it came in a swift dive,
with a chilling cry into my aging slumber

    as if I were a hare,
    nesting on the prairie;
    its iron-grey claws

        piercing my heart
        so fiercely
        I could not breathe;

            sealing its seed
            deep in my blood;
            eyeing me, then

releasing me on this threshold,
to hold this day yet more ardently.

The Reunion

He is up to watch the sunrise, on the slow
uphill run; the dining-car breakfast — coffee,
bacon and eggs. How had she found his number,
Class of '52. Charles, *you really must come.*
It won't be a reunion without you.

Only now does he begin to recall the jock talk:
kike, cunt, faggot. The bullies who taunted Fran
on her way home from school. She never came back.
The Torres boys, blackballed from the youth group:
the dads said their names and their church were bad.

His doctor was reported to the FBI:
He talks like a Commie, loves
Russian music and plays it on his fiddle, too.
The soulful howl of the train
told him how alone he had become.

The yip of coyotes, running in the sage,
you'll never fit in. The train stops
at his destination. He hesitates. Replaces
his suitcase, and ambles back to the club car,
picks up the morning's *Los Angeles Times*,

sees a notice that the Philharmonic will play
the Shostakovich No.10 in E minor tonight.
I hope it is not too late to get in. And then,
as crisply and clearly as this frosty morning,
he remembers boarding that train

sixty years ago today, and how he sat
looking out his window, while before him
a single rose in a vase trembled
as the train, swaying gently around the bend,
took him to where he had never been.

Why would you ever go back.

Seamus Heaney

On that wind-full night, the hall
was full to hear your voice,
and I was keen to listen, but
your words, your brogue, came
blurred, my hearing clogged,

so that I heard a wordless ocean;
I heard the voice of waves
which swayed my boat of skin,
tolled my bones;

I heard a deeper sound which
took me into a sea uncharted
and free.

And still I hear your ocean call
as on that wind-full night,
and now I have your books;
charts to sail me home.

Singular

Looking back over your life you can see
how you seldom fit in; how you often found yourself
out of line, and how paying attention was a challenge

you chose not to manage. If you were asked
'black' or 'white', you saw fifty-seven
shades of gray; and always chose

the odd one out. Going straight
home gave way to a different path,
and you chose your own counsel

over what was common lore. You did not
choose to be contrary, yet you could always
disagree, and because the easy track was not your way,

you paid for it, over and over,
and loneliness was your wage,
and aloneness your trove.

You may never see eye to eye, and a lie
gives chilling refuge. You have no call to deceive,
nor need to deny what you believe.

You have, by any count, reached the age
of consent, and you shall choose
which views to hold, and which to lose.

Looking back over your life you can claim
your very oddness, was no curse;
it is life's gift, life's holy trust.

Song of Longing

Far above the stubbed corn field, their calls
pierce the sheer fall sky: a skein of Canada
geese move higher and faster. They've caught
the first Manitoba Clipper for their flight south.
Their purpose steadfast. They're on their way home.

The Sandhill Cranes, last week, circled the field,
landed and took off, repeating the exercise
as if checking their equipment before
the great flight. Their raucous calls to another land.

The crows are more business-like. They poke about
to see if there is anything here that they've left
behind which they might want to take with them.
With one last look to be sure everything
is in order, they take off to the not-so-far south.

The nasturtium still waits at my door, does not shrivel,
survives the bite of 28 degrees Fahrenheit
as insistent and beaming as it was in August.
It longs for this life, in this world, never to end.

At night I lay and listen to a song
of longing, as it writes itself in me,
for peace, for the homeless, the starving,
for the destruction of this world to end.

Five Sea Interludes

> *— using lines from Mary Rose O'Reilly,*
> 'Half-Wild'

I.

The sea is my mother,
who draws me to herself,
who *surprises the presences*
within me, brings
to surface secrets
kept from myself.
Each wave echoes within.
In my blood is the taste and love
of the sea. A life given
without fee. I carry her ghosts
and history. In her sighs
I know my mother's voice.

II.

I knew them up close. I carried
them within myself, giving them their
rhythm as only a rocking crooning
mother can do. Debussy could
not hear my music until he went
inland, and there my voices,
my rhythms came true.

III.

I will hear in the sea's naming
all of my parts, elbow
to draw the bow, ankle,
the angle binding leg and foot.
The psalmist in praise says,
*fearfully and wonderfully am I
made.* You know all and call each
to yourself.

IV.

The sea, *shook by her longing
to break* from where she has lived,
returns to the earth in rain and snow,
offers herself, again and again, to give
life.

As a mother
forever yearns for her children,
will she return to cover the earth?

V.

In the end *I have surrendered
to longing.* The sea lives in me
as presences. Its absences
make it only more clear.
Make it rock my skin boat,
draw me on, draw me on.

Goshawk

It is a rare warm day for late October.
He is perched on the old fencepost,
unnoticed by the traffic hurtling by below.
He has grown to ignore that mindless,
hellbent-for-nowhere, madness.

Today he is content with the sun
warming his back. No longer
does he envy the lofty circles
of the haughty bald eagle, far above.

What thoughts does an old goshawk
have when the day is so perfect?
Perhaps he's caught in the glory
and beauty of everything in his sight.
Maybe he's hopelessly enraptured

in the fall colors, the red sumac,
the rusty scrub oak. Or maybe
he has a bliss spirit, which is always
in awe of the all. He's an old bird, you know.

His feathers, not as sleek and shiny as they were.
His eyesight, not as keen. Once
he was fast enough to rush through the trees
to catch and crush a hare hopelessly unaware.
At his age, he's not given to nostalgia

or regret, as some are in their senescence. He is pure intent, that single-mindedness admired by the sages. His problem:
What was it I was to bring back to the nest?

A Thing with Feathers

— *Emily Dickinson*

Its life is never
without care. Always alert,
exit flight rehearsed.

The red finch flies up,
flutters in midair, then grasps
a perch at the cedar feeder. A grackle
muscles in. Two blue jays jockey up.
A red-winged blackbird flashes through,
changes the scene.

A red finch
must carry caution deep
within.

Still, as a Child

Hidden on the north side of our gray garage,
nested in a volunteer elm next to the wall,
is a red-crowned finch. Not moving,

watching me. Does he sense that I shall do no
harm, or is he snared by fear. Not moving,
I stand while our eyes touch. Carefully,

I withdraw. He stays.

I return to the nest made from twigs, bits
of cellophane and red thread, intricately woven,
to see if there are blue eggs, or

nestlings craning to be fed. It is bare.
I watch for his return to set up housekeeping
on this gentle edge of the world.

He has not. Yet, still,

I wait. Yet I wait,
still, as a child.

The Vanishing Art of Feather Reading

The child, at the age of four,
reads me a feather she found on the trail
to the hidden pond. She reads it to me
as a wise crone might read ancient runes,
when everyone else who once read this tongue
has long since forgotten how. She reads
fluently as she points to each part of the feather,
and describes lost kingdoms, princesses, rivers
to be crossed, treasures to be found, and
a caged unicorn. To me it is as complicated
as reading tea leaves, the tarot, or one's DNA.
No detail too small not to describe, she reads
on until the entire story is told.

Six years later, I hear her sing the part
of a beautiful young princess held in a tower
in her school play.

O, child, do not ever lose
the art of feather reading.

Paradise

The thief made it there
in a day.

The harlots and tax collectors
got in ahead of the righteous.

When the preacher told me
who gets in and who is locked out,
I knew it was an outright lie.

Kids get in free.
It's easier for them to see.

If I blunder in unannounced,
and there are empty stares
of shock. Sorry. I did not knock.
I'll find my way out.

They say there are no tears
in paradise. If they are right
it is no place for me.

Jesus said it is within us,
among us. The Buddha: it is here
hidden in plain view.

For Norman Lear it is in that space
between *over* and *next*. In-between
is a hammock. The present moment.

If there is a gate there, it is open,
and the key is long lost.

Vissi d'arte, Vissi d'amore

Once again Tosca sings *Vissi d'arte,*
but the child does not want it to end.

He pleads with his mother, *Play it again.*
She consents, and, with Tosca,
he sings to make her song his own.

Ungrateful child. Impossible child.
He points to his mother: *Stay away!*
because he knows he must be alone.

He was the child who, when the others
had finished the maypole dance, always
added another step or two, and when
their song was over, he began another.

I am the child who gazed out the window
when the teacher called his name, the one
always on the wrong page, but knew
the correct answer to the question never asked.

I am the child
who sang,
I lived for art.
I lived for love.

I am the one
who does not
want it to end.

I Will Leave It Free And Open And Unnamed

— Dorothea Lasky, "There is no name yet"

I closed the door behind me
and stepped into the first day
of spring. I am leaving
and some things must be left
behind: those well-fingered stones
of hurt and anger. I'll have no use
for them where I'll be going. Instead,
I'll carry those memories
light enough to buoy me
on the way ahead.

I leave with that sense one has
on a ferry
when where one has been,
slowly, and finally,
moves away. And where one stands
oblivious to what lies ahead.

That other voice,
the one deep within,
the one I must trust the most,
tells me, this day you gave
yourself a priceless gift.

I will leave it free
and open
and unnamed.

Wayfarer

Mid-morning, winter,
bitter clear, near blinding;

in the distance,
seven wild turkeys
making their way through the field,

away from their island roost
of elm and sumac, brush and ash.

What is it I seek this winter's day?

I follow the turkeys over a crest
to where the west wind has swept

the ground snow-bare,
where soybean stems appear

and the turkeys feed
on their scanty hoard of beans

disregarded in the fall harvest.

Sisyphus

Camus said the story is a metaphor
for the absurdity of life. Poor Sisyphus
had never in his life even picked up a rock.

He was a poet. The people in his village
would greet him with their wry grins,
Hey Siph, you still writing po-e-try.

He learned to ignore them, but
sometimes, when he felt he had written
his best, he'd read it out loud.
Then he'd shout,
This one is shit!

Of course you know the story.
You know what the duffer does
the very next morning.

Mercy

If you are thrown out
of your home, she
brings you into her own.
She knows what it means
to have no place to go.
She gives you her coat
when you have lost your
only one. She stays up
late with you when you
grieve. She doesn't leave
the room when you rage;
she listens even more.
She will hear you when no one
else will give it a try.
She brings you hot soup
when you are sick and even
when you're not — thought
you just might like it. If you are new
in town, she shows you around.
She is first in line to forgive you,
even before you knew to ask.
She doesn't hold a grudge,
she knows it belongs in the trash.
Mercy seeks you out when you're
alone in a crowd. She knows
how it is to feel out of place.
She doesn't need to get ahead —

she's content to walk at your side.
She doesn't have to be right.
She wants to hear your side.
Don't ask her for the score,
she doesn't know, nor care. While
I write this, she smiles and says,
Keep on, I know you can do it.
As the day ends, just before you
fall asleep, listen. Hear her whisper,
Merci!

What Do You Bear?

The gray morning snow hesitates.
The wintry traffic slows, then stops.
Across the abandoned, ice rutted, parking lot,
you make your way. Although you teeter,
almost stumble, you follow the route
I have seen you take before.
Why don't you find a safer way?
All of the clothes you own are on
your back. As though you are guiding
two children across the icy way,
you carry two low hanging plastic bags,
which hold all you've got.

What do you bear that is so precious
you cannot live without it?

You keep to your solitary path
as the snow slowly starts again,
and the traffic begins to move,
like a cortege, moving me on. At
the corner I take a turn to the right
as if to go around the block,
to give you a lift,
which I never do.

What Is Poetry, and Where Do I Fit In?

Souvenirs

From the Latin, *sub venire*, 'occur to the mind'.
From my traumatized, digitally challenged,
segmented, fragmented, colonized being,
it is a risky test to reveal my shy and wild, secret and
silent, most precious, utterly true self. No trophies,
no awards, only gaudy truth; no words barred; only
this blood stained, sweat infused life.

Embellishment

From the Latin, *bellus*, 'handsome, beautiful'. If Venus
adorns the sky at its most azure, and the gold of forsythias
sings spring is here; if a beauty mark obsesses the eye,
and a stutter heightens attention in the ear, and if the Pleiades
and Orion embellish the clear, crisp autumn night,
and near-death reminds us how dear is our life, then
poetry stuns and bejewels the banality of our minds.

Monetary Investment

From the Latin, *moneta*, 'money', and *investire*, 'to clothe'.
At my age the practical wisdom is to invest with prudence.
With little money, and less to invest, I have decided to live
abundantly with the vanishing time I have left. Spendthrift
that I am, and not given to the practical way, I have taken
risky, unexplored paths. What dignity I ever had is spent.
And my pride is an empty bank. I fling it all for tart poetry.

Status Symbol

From the Greek, *statis*, 'standing', and *symbolon*, 'token of identity'. What do you have to show for yourself? Where is your proof? These scribbles and scraps do show. Words lobbed at paper like Jackson Pollock threw his oils. Maybe a happening. Maybe Lady Luck will be a lady tonight. I leave these souvenirs, part epigraph, part strikings and plumbings. I learned poetry from the best. *I'm nobody! Who are you?*

Why We're Here

The sky is grey, the field lies fallow.
Winter hangs on and spring is held
at bay, Two women walk side by side
one in green the other in red, mother
and daughter, Jen and Ann. From where
I watch I can't hear what they say. Both
women are nurses. Jen suffers from
autoimmune hepatitis. Has for years. If she
does not receive a liver transplant soon,
she will die. The daughter wants to risk,
give her mother what her mother
has given her. They're perfectly matched.
Jen aches with the disease, agonizes
over the risks for her daughter,
the rightness of doing this to save
her own life. Jen, strong as steel,
never given to nonsense, once,
over the fence, told me, *I believe
we're here on earth to help each other.*

A sharp cold wind comes.
They walk closer together.

The Wind in the Night

The hum of the night wind carried him
back to the weathered white church,
up its unsteady steps, where the outside
door was never locked, and the inside
doors breathed the restive desert wind
in and out, and scents of candle wax
and incense were held in tenebrous light
and a red sanctuary light hung,
a sentinel of an unseen presence. There

in the back, on a well-worn pew
a young man sits, alone, neither a seeker
nor a believer, more like a refugee
from an alien country, waiting passage
to an unknown shore. It is silence

that has drawn him
to this place over and over again:
silence which is not an absence
of sound, for he knows its creaks and sighs;
instead it is an enfoldment like the silence
that holds all music in its matrix;
a presence that envelops him
creating a consonance within him
he has never known before.

And suddenly he realizes,
I have come home.

The old haunt long since razed,
replaced by a new structure,
square and locked except for meetings,
like a union hall or a lodge,
then closed, like a bank,
its cold bolt thrown.

To Wonder

As I now have the leisure, I might wonder
if my life has not been a riddled puzzle. Is it too
late to fit the pieces together. Is there any wisdom
to be found before I go under. May I measure
my life like a bookkeeper, scrupulously looking for
errors that might be corrected. I approach the age

of eighty. Am I too late to revise. My age
gives no certified warranty. Yet I still wonder
as if I were that dreamy child of four,
rolling on the green, keen to see
the sky's buffalo herds, and in the thunder
heard them run. Might wisdom

open me to life's elusive treasure. Is there any wisdom
under the sun. Are we entering another dark age.
Let me tell you what I have uncovered. The measure
of life is not in years or gains. It is in wonder
itself, where each moment is a gift, freely offered to
cherish, relish, to taste and see.

Each day is its own eternity; an instant is forever.
It is its liminal richness, it is its own wisdom,
and nothing shall devalue its currency. I know, too,
the gift of life is fecklessly flushed away in our age;
life plundered for vapid treasures. Is it any wonder
our pace becomes more rapid with each failed measure.

Receive life as a gift never to be mortgaged. Don't measure
or compare yourself to any other. Your life is for
more than debits and credits. I offer my life to wonder,
whose light I, only now, begin to sing. True wisdom
is waiting in the glory of the ordinary. This age
would buy us with its crisp counterfeit tender. To

time's double-handed tricks I shall give no creed. Too,
counting and assessing give me no good measure,
for I have received an infinite treasure. The age
I am given is not for restless introspection, nor for
buyer's remorse. I stake my claim on child's wisdom
for which there is no price: the gift of life is wonder.

Ask not what I am up to, or what my life is for.
There is no measure. If I have any wisdom,
any tonic for my age, it is this cup brimming with wonder.

Like a Bell

At eighty,
or close to,
I am not
the man
I once was
or thought
I should be.
No longer
can I do
what I
once did,
nor do I
care to.
Instead
it is poetry
that turns
my head.
This is not
senescence,
as you might
suspect,
so do not
give me your
omniscient
grin. Today

I slip through
the needle's
eye, and grasp
the treasure,
hidden
in the field,
waiting
for me.
Don't you
see it? It is
clear to me,
like a bell,

like a bell.

Itasca

—for Jana

Come with me to Lake Itasca in late autumn
when the colors of the leaves sing,
when the sun's light has softened

and the gold and silver shine
glory into that sylvan world.
And we shall sit and listen

to the lull of the lake
as its waters slip into the stream
and begins its sacred journey—

becomes the river, moves through the delta,
joins the ocean. We shall rise, our feet bare,
and step into the water,

our bodies washed,
and we shall float
into the unknown sea.

While I Have Time

I play my rhapsody.
although I hold no first chair.
My solo is played
on this plain birch table.
My score is a one-part
invention
written
in this blue
composition book.
The baton, yellow
and pointed,
leads me with trembling
direction.

My days
grow shorter.
I am married,
even so,
to this world.

Mortal,

— for Jana

of course I am, yet I hesitate.
It is fancy that gives the pause;
for no matter how hard I try
to imagine it, there is always
a *me*, no matter how minuscule
or obscure I become. Perhaps
it is that I shall exit this stage,
yet remain behind the curtain,
and watch the show go on,
an unobserved observer.

But you.

The stage
is changed
when you appear.
Cut me through,
but do not
leave me
here
without you.

Portal

In solitude I write, in a corner
ten-by-ten loft whose windows, facing south
and west into fierce woods and fields, oversee
a family of four white-tailed deer, a lonely
gray wolf and a gang of coyotes. Overhead,
as I watch, a red-tailed hawk considers
a young cotton tail. This portal

is a refuge for royal migrants
on their north and south flights:
warblers and grosbeaks, orioles
and tanagers and Sandhill cranes,
and on the pond, silent and solemn, stands
the great blue heron. Here, the sun
sets, rises, brings spring
and fall equinoxes; solstices
bring heat and humidity;
bitter cold and ineffable lucidity.
Snowfall. Rain. Sleet and hail.
The moon waxes and wanes, rises
to it zenith, then sets.
The Milky Way swings me into
my vertiginous home. Elms and maples soar,
and embrace my eyrie; their new leaves
grow viridescent, then turn luminous
flaxen-gold, lofted by the north wind,
to become gray-brown shrouds

against the earth. My body
and mind, with the shaky
sensitivity of an old compass,
explores and discovers
what I have slowly learned.

These awkward and simple markings
of a body electrified with life
given to be lived boldly
without warranty, or refund.
I write, oh, more fiercely, every day —
every day and each day a holy day.

This Day

I want to sit on this weathered gray bench,
on the end of this cedar dock, with the morning
sun just this warm, with this gentle wind,

and I want to feel these shiftless waves
on this lake, and just hang like these clouds
with nothing better to do, where an odd call

of gull or caw of crow is just enough for me.
I want to sit here until I am bored to the bone
until my thoughts slow down like this small blue boat

moored here, beside me, then maybe, maybe,
I might want to get some thing done,
but for now I listen as a loon calls my name.

ACKNOWLEDGMENTS

To Jana Marie Bollman, wife and the light and joy of my life. Each day through these fifty-four years you give me your love, your encouragement, and your wisdom. And now you give me daily support to write.

To my daughters Meg and Kate, you are always ready to hear a new poem and give me your hearts.

To the Sisters of St. Benedict's Monastery, St. Joseph, you feed me daily with your beautiful life, always ready to show me true hospitality.

To J. Weston Smith and the late Marilyn Colby Smith who encouraged me to write years before I would write a poem. Marilyn, in her last days you asked me to bring new poems to your bedside. You introduced me as *Charlie, he's a real poet.*

To the Fireroast Poets, my poetry group loving me these past seven years: Mary Broderick, Sue Crouse, Barb Draper, Doug Freeman, and Naomi Jackson. Your lives and poems bring me joy.

To Jude Nutter, your patience and understanding brought this old man step by step, to write poetry. You always saw the poem I was trying to write.

To Barb Draper, aka, Calamity Jane, you spurred me on to do this book and carefully read through all of my poems.

To Leslie Matton-Flynn, your genius made this book a work of art, 'a book to hold and to behold.'

To Sr. Mara Faulkner, OSB, teacher extraordinaire, you read the first draft and gave it direction and praise.

To Deborah Keenan, your inspired teaching prompted most of the poems in 'Portals'. You saw much more than I knew was there. Deborah, you are ever generous, magnanimous, encouraging and challenge me to do more than I had ever imagined possible.

To you readers of my poems who have found messages in them meant just for you. Yes, I have been blessed with wonderful readers and teachers, mentors who have helped me read poetry, love poetry, and write each day with a spirit of delight. These poems are not perfect, but that is not what poetry is about. At the age of eighty 'Portals' is my testament, and yet I feel as if I have only just begun.

PORTALS

ISBN 978-0-9852692-3-4

Printed in the United States of America

Copyright © 2017 by Charles Wm. Preble

All rights reserved. No part of this book may be reproduced in any form by any electronic or mechanical means including photocopying, recording, or information storage and retrieval without permission in writing from the authors.

For permissions and information contact
Charles Preble, P.O. Box 844, Saint Joseph, MN 56374

Book design and layout: Leslie Matton-Flynn, Cup and Spiral Books, Minneapolis, MN
Editor: Leslie Matton-Flynn
Cover image: Charles Wm. Preble